Contents

© SUSAETA EDICIONES, S.A.
C/Campezo, 13 – 28022 Madrid, Spain
Tel.: +34 91 3009100 – Fax: +34 91 3009118
www.susaeta.com
© 2015 Brown Watson, England
Reprinted 2015
ISBN: 978 0 7097 2234 2
Printed in Malaysia

Bible Stories for Children

Text by Silvia Alonso

Illustrations by Manuel Galiana

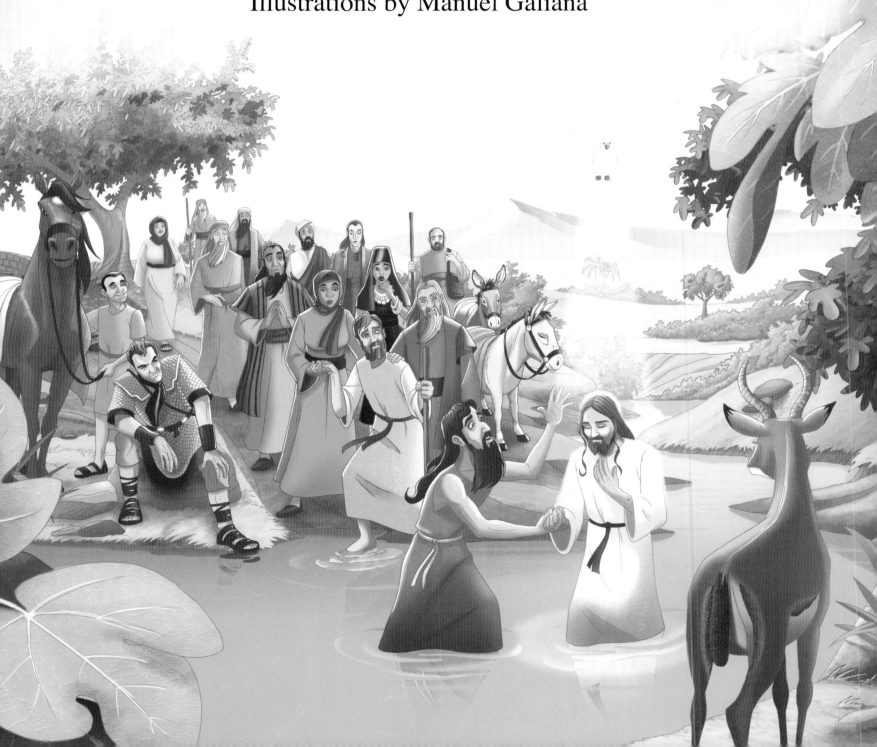

CREATION – ADAM AND EVE

In the beginning, everything was darkness, and God thought that something should change. So He invented light and separated it from darkness, and created day and night. He also thought that it would be good if there were different spaces, so He separated the sky and the water and left a dry area, the Earth. On it He made plants, flowers, trees and fruit appear. In the sky He placed the sun, the moon and the stars. He also created the birds for the sky, the fish for the seas and the other animals for the land.

On the sixth day, God decided to make humans; they would be like him and would rule over all the fish, the birds and the animals. He modelled a man using dust from the ground and breathed life into him. The man was called Adam and God built a beautiful garden for him and called it Eden, so that he could live there and have everything he needed. But God realised Adam needed some company and He made Eve from one of Adam's ribs. After working for six days on his new world without stopping, on the seventh day God rested, satisfied with His work.

Adam and Eve lived happily in the Garden of Eden, surrounded by their friends, the animals. They could eat from all of the trees in the garden, except for one, the Tree of the Knowledge of Good and Evil. God had warned them about this tree:
"Don't taste its fruit or you will be punished."

One day, a serpent tricked them and made Eve eat from the forbidden tree. She saw how good it was and told Adam to try some. God was very angry. He threw them out of the Garden of Eden and stopped them from returning. "Now you will have to work for your food and nothing will ever be easy for you," He said.

NOAH'S ARK

As the years passed, there were more and more humans on the Earth. God watched them and saw that they were bad. There was only one, called Noah, who He was happy with, and He decided to give him a job to do:

"I am going to make it rain for forty days so that everything is flooded. To save yourself, build a boat out of wood, an ark, and live in it with your family and two of every kind of animal that exists."

The storm God spoke about arrived and everything was covered in water. Many days passed before the rain stopped. One day, Noah sent out a dove and it returned carrying a branch of an olive tree in its beak.
"It has found somewhere to perch!" he exclaimed.
When Noah and his family arrived on dry land, they got out of the ark with all of the animals. God told them He would never flood the whole Earth again, and as a symbol of His promise, he drew a rainbow in the sky.

THE TOWER OF BABEL

Centuries after the flood, there were many descendants of Noah on the Earth. They were one single community, where the people all spoke the same language and travelled with their herds of animals. One day, they arrived at a very beautiful place and decided to stay there. They made clay bricks and built houses for everyone, and they created a great city. The people were so proud that they felt like they could do anything:

"We will build a tower so tall that it reaches Heaven."

God was saddened that the people were so proud and wanted to do things their own way, and He decided to confuse them. Suddenly, they could not understand each other: they were speaking different languages!

And so they stopped building the tower, which was called Babel, meaning "confusion". They could no longer live together on the same land and they went to different parts of the world.

ABRAHAM

Abraham was a good man and for that reason God watched over him. One day He asked him to leave the place where he lived with his wife, Sarah, to go on a very long journey to a beautiful place called Canaan. "There I will give you children and they will bear many more, until there are as many as the stars in the sky."
But the years passed, and Sarah, who was already old, had not become pregnant.

One day, God sent three men to Abraham's house. He treated them with great respect, even though he did not know who they were.
"You are going to be a mother," they told Sarah.
She laughed because she thought that she was too old to have children, but after nine months, Isaac was born, just as she had been promised. Abraham did not know it, but many years later, one of his descendants would give birth to Jesus Christ.

MOSES

Centuries later, many Israelites, who were the descendants of Abraham, lived in Egypt. There were so many that the Egyptians were afraid that they would become stronger than them and so they made them slaves. But their numbers continued to grow and Pharaoh ordered that all newborn baby boys were to be killed.

However, one Hebrew mother, after having her baby, wanted to save it. She floated him down the river in a basket of reeds, trusting that her son would be kept safe. The little basket was found by the Pharaoh's daughter who was bathing in the river, and when she saw him, she said sadly:

"He must be an abandoned Israelite child. I will take care of him." She called him Moses and he was raised in the palace. One day, young Moses killed an Egyptian to defend a Hebrew man. He knew that he had to escape from Egypt.

THE PLAGUES OF EGYPT

Moses became a shepherd in a far-off land. One day, God asked him to return to Egypt to save his people from slavery and to guide them to a safe place. Moses asked Pharaoh to free the Israelites, but he refused and ordered them to work even harder still. But God gave Moses power to perform miracles with his staff and sent plagues over Egypt, one for every time Pharaoh said "no".

He turned the water in the river into blood, thousands of frogs, gnats and flies appeared; He brought disease, sores, a hailstorm, a plague of locusts and three days of night. These plagues left the population without fish, crops or livestock, and also caused great unrest. But Pharaoh always said no. The tenth plague was the worst: all of the firstborn sons of the Egyptians died. This time, Pharaoh ordered all of the Israelites to leave Egypt.

THE TEN COMMANDMENTS

Thousands of Israelites finally left Egypt, guided by Moses.
But Pharaoh, who changed his mind straight away and
did not want to let them go, followed them with his
army. God warned Moses, and when they arrived at
the Red Sea, Moses lifted his staff and the water parted
so that the Israelites could pass through, but fell back
again so that all the Egyptian army were drowned.
The Israelites continued walking for many days through
the Sinai Desert, until they reached the mountain there.

Moses climbed to the highest point of the mountain to listen to the voice of God that called to him. The Lord gave him ten rules, which were written by Him and carved with His finger into two stone tablets. These rules were for the people to learn and follow, and are known as the Ten Commandments.

THE WALLS OF JERICHO

The journey through the desert was very long and Moses died shortly before reaching the Promised Land. Joshua took command. The first city they reached when they left the desert was Jericho. It was surrounded by tall, thick walls and its people, who were scared of the Israelites, had closed the gates to stop them from entering the city. God helped them once again, telling them what they should do.

For six days all the Israelites walked slowly around the city walls once. Seven priests blew trumpets made from rams' horns but everyone else was quiet. On the seventh day they did the same thing except they went around seven times. Then there was a long trumpet blast and everyone else shouted very loudly. They made such a deafening noise that the walls fell down as if they were made of paper.

SAMSON

Samson was a Hebrew who was so incredibly strong that nobody could beat him. He was capable of defeating a lion with his bare hands, or ripping out and lifting up a heavy gate, as well as other amazing things. The Philistines, who were his enemies, decided to capture him, but to do this they needed to know the secret of his strength.

Samson fell in love with a Philistine called Delilah. Samson's enemies convinced her to find out his secret. She nagged him so much he finally told her:

"If you cut my hair, I will lose my strength."
Delilah cut his hair and the Philistines made him a slave. But they did not
notice that his hair had grown again, and when he recovered his strength,
Samson destroyed their temple, pushing over the pillars with his hands.
It was his last act, as he died under the rubble.

DAVID AND GOLIATH

The Philistines and the Israelites were at war and the armies spent days standing in two lines, facing each other. In the Philistine camp there was an enormous man called Goliath, who was nearly ten feet tall and dressed in bronze armour. Every day he shouted:
"Choose someone to fight against me; if he defeats me, our people will be your slaves." But everyone was afraid of him and no one dared to fight him.

David was a shepherd who carried messages and provisions to his brothers who served in the Israelite army. One day he heard of Goliath's challenge. "Nobody is invincible. I will fight him with God's help."
As he was young and inexperienced, nobody believed he could win. Goliath laughed to see him without armour and with only a slingshot in his hand, but David fired a stone and it hit him right in the forehead, knocking him over. Seeing that Goliath was defeated, the Philistine army fled.

SOLOMON

Solomon was one of the Israelite kings and God had given him the gift of wisdom. One day, two women with a baby came to see the king. One of them said: "This woman's son died, so she stole mine and swapped it for her dead child." "She's lying!" shouted the other woman. "My son is the one that is alive and she switched them."

Solomon asked to be brought a sword and ordered:
"Cut the child in two and give half to each of the mothers."
One of them agreed with the decision. The other burst into tears, saying to Solomon:
"I would prefer that the child lived and stayed with this other woman. Please don't kill him."
And so the king declared:
"Give the child to the second mother, because this is her son."

THE BIRTH OF JESUS

God sent an angel to the town of Nazareth to speak to a young girl called Mary:

"You are going to have a baby boy and you will give him the name Jesus. He will be the Son of God and will reign for ever and ever."

Although she was engaged to Joseph, Mary was not married and was very surprised to find out that she was going to be a virgin mother. The angel also appeared to Joseph and explained everything to him. A little while later they got married.

At that time, the emperor who ruled wanted to know how many people lived in his empire and all of the people had to register in the city where they were born.

"We have to go to Bethlehem, the city that I come from," Joseph explained to Mary, when her son was about to be born.

When they arrived, they could not find a place to sleep and they stayed in a stable for animals. Jesus was born there, and was laid in a manger.

THE WISE MEN

Some wise men who were studying the stars saw a very bright one in the sky which they hadn't seen before. In their books they read that this meant that a new king had been born, and they wanted to meet him.

The wise men followed the light of the star from the East, which led them to Jerusalem.

"Where is the newborn who will be king of the Jews?" they asked. But nobody knew what to tell them.

The rumour about the new king also reached the ears of Herod, who ruled the land. All of the talk about there being a new king made him fear for his power. After finding out that Jesus was in Bethlehem, he informed the wise men, hiding his evil intentions: "When you find him, let me know. I would also like to meet him."

In Bethlehem, the wise men followed the star and found Jesus, and gave him gifts of gold, frankincense and myrrh. In a dream, God warned them: "Don't return to Herod's palace."

THE CHILDHOOD OF JESUS

When he realised he could not find Jesus, Herod ordered all of the boys under the age of two to be killed, to make sure that the new Jewish king would die:

"I will be the only king."

But Mary and Joseph, warned by God, fled with the child and made a home in Egypt. When Herod died, they returned to Nazareth. Jesus grew up in this town where he helped Joseph in his carpenter's workshop and learned to read in the synagogue.

When he was twelve years old, he went with his parents to Jerusalem to celebrate Passover. Afterwards, on the journey home, Mary and Joseph realised Jesus was missing. They were very worried and went back to the city to look until they found him in the temple, surrounded by teachers. They were all listening and marvelling at the insight of such a young boy.

THE BAPTISM AND DISCIPLES OF JESUS

While Jesus became an adult in Nazareth, his cousin John prepared the people for the arrival of a new leader. John lived in the desert. Many people went to listen to him and to be baptised by him in the River Jordan. This was a symbol of their sins being washed away. One day, Jesus also went to be baptised. When he left the water, the sky opened and the Spirit of God, in the form of a dove, landed on Jesus. A voice came from the sky: "This is my Son, I am pleased with him."

After this, Jesus lived in the desert for forty days with nothing to eat. The devil tried to tempt Jesus to follow him and not God, but he did not succeed. When he left the desert, Jesus went to the fishing villages of Galilee to tell the people to turn back to God. News about him spread, and many people went to meet him and wanted to hear what he had to say. From those who followed him, he chose twelve men to be his disciples.

THE MIRACLES OF JESUS

Jesus performed some amazing miracles using his hands and his words, to demonstrate the wonders that God was capable of through Him. His first miracle took place during some wedding celebrations in Cana, when, after all the drinks had been finished, he turned jugs of water into delicious wine for the guests.

Another time, some men brought a paralysed man on a stretcher to Jesus. "Get up and walk." commanded Jesus. And the man could walk without help.

One day, Jesus went to the beach. He was surrounded by thousands of people who had come to see him; they were hungry and they could only find five loaves of bread and two fishes. Jesus divided the bread and the fishes and, amazingly, as he and the disciples handed it out, there was enough food for everyone. On another day, a man called Lazarus had died after an illness. When Jesus arrived at his tomb, he said: "Lazarus, come out!"
And the man came out, alive and well.

THE LAST SUPPER AND THE ARREST OF JESUS

The news of the miracles and the teachings of Jesus meant that many people followed him, but there were also others who were afraid of losing power because of him. They planned to have him arrested and killed. They were pleased when Judas, one of Jesus' twelve disciples, told them he would hand Jesus over to them, and they promised to give him some money. One evening, soon after, Jesus was celebrating the Passover with his twelve disciples. He was sad. God had told him that he would die and he knew that this would be his last supper.

During the meal they broke bread, and Jesus said:
"Take this and eat; this bread is my body." Then wine was served in a chalice:
"Everyone drink; this wine is the blood that I will shed when I die for the good
of all men."
Before finishing the dinner, Jesus foretold: "Tonight, one of you will betray me
and will hand me over." After this, Jesus went to pray on the Mount of Olives;
then some soldiers arrived, accompanied by Judas, and captured him.

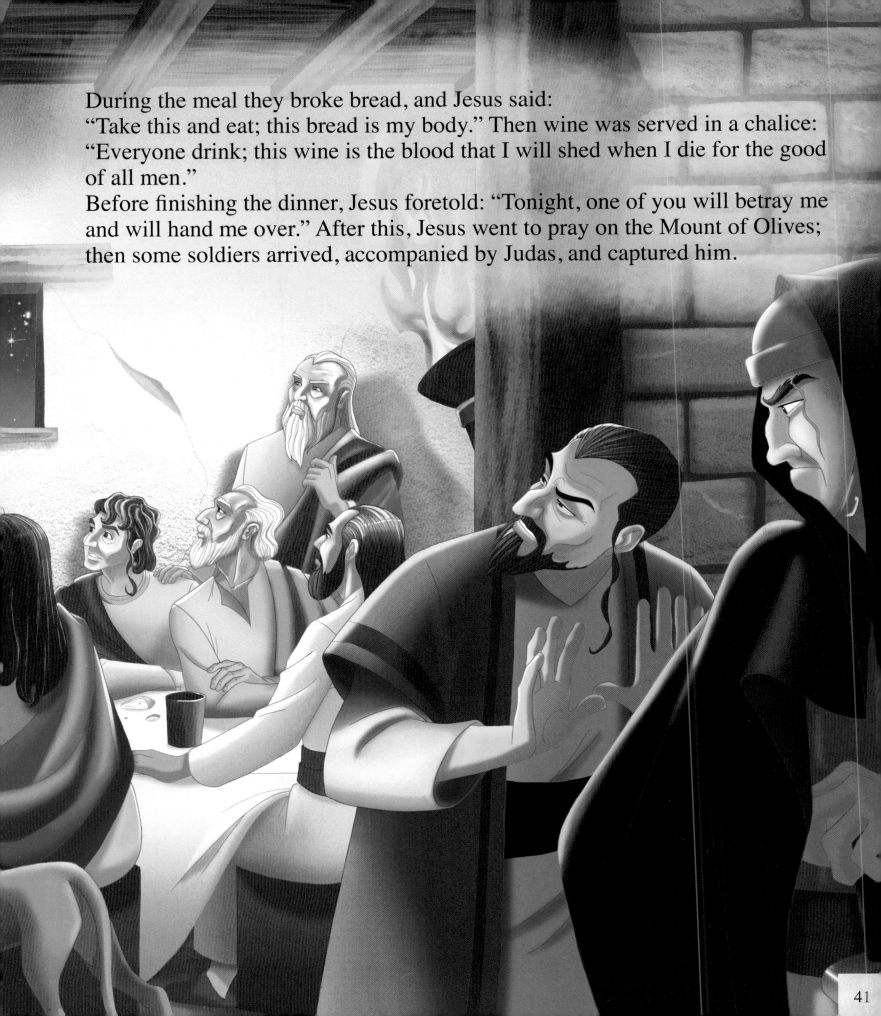

SENTENCING AND CRUCIFIXION

The soldiers tied Jesus up and took him to the high priest's house and then at daybreak to the whole council to pass judgement on him. There, they asked him:

"Do you confirm that you are the Son of God?"

"I am."

"Saying this is an offence to God: you deserve to die," they decided. Then, they brought him before Pilate, the governor, to confirm the death sentence.

After he had interrogated him, Pilate knew that Jesus had not done anything wrong, but was afraid of the crowd who were demanding his death. They were shouting "Crucify him!" This was how the Romans executed their prisoners.

And so Pilate gave Jesus to them. The soldiers whipped him. As a joke, they made him wear a red cloak and a crown of thorns, as if he were a king, and they forced him to carry his cross the whole way to the hill where he would be crucified.

43

DEATH AND RESURRECTION

They nailed Jesus to the cross and kept watch over him there. The moment before he died, everything suddenly went dark, even though it was the middle of the day. "My Lord, why have you abandoned me?" he cried before he died.

That night Jesus' friends took his body from the cross and wrapped it in a sheet. Pilate gave them permission to take it. They put Jesus' body in a tomb inside a cave, which was their custom, and closed the entrance with a big rock.

Three days later, Mary Magdalene, a follower of Jesus, went to visit the tomb. She found that the rock in front of the entrance had been moved and the tomb was empty. At first she thought that somebody had taken the body, but when she looked inside again, an angel appeared:
"Do not be afraid. Jesus has been raised from the dead and is going to be reunited with God, his Father." Then Jesus appeared to her and said:
"Please tell my disciples I'm alive, and tell them they will find me in Galilee."